AR Book Level: 5.9
Point Value: 2.0
Quiz No. 65803
Interest Level: MG

GREAT MOMENTS
AT THE OLYMPICS

By Joanne and James Mattern

Library
Renfroe Middle School
220 W. College Ave.
Decatur, GA 30030

Perfection Learning®

About the Authors

Joanne Mattern is the author of many books for children. She especially likes writing nonfiction because it allows her to bring real people, places, and events to life. "I firmly believe that everything in the world is a story waiting to be told."

Along with writing, Joanne enjoys speaking to school and community groups about the topics in her books. She is also a huge baseball fan and enjoys music and needlework.

Joanne's husband, James, enjoys all sports. He is especially interested in sports history, trivia, and statistics.

Joanne and James live in the Hudson Valley of New York State with their young daughter. The family also includes a greyhound and two cats. "More animals are always welcome!"

Design: Emily J. Greazel

Image Credits: © CARON/CORBIS SYGMA: cover; © Reuters NewMedia Inc./CORBIS: pp. 5, 22–23, 36–37, 44; © Bettmann/CORBIS: pp. 8, 26–27; © Duomo/CORBIS: pp. 19, 47; © AFP/CORBIS: pp. 39, 52

ArtToday (some images copyright www.arttoday.com): pp. 4, 6, 10, 15, 28–29, 32, 34, 41; Corel Professional Photos: 12, 53, 54, 57, 58

Text © 2003 by Perfection Learning® Corporation.
All rights reserved. No part of this book may be reproduced, stored in a retrieval system, or transmitted in any form or by any means, electronic, mechanical, photocopying, recording, or otherwise, without prior permission of the publisher.
Printed in the United States of America. For information, contact Perfection Learning® Corporation, 1000 North Second Avenue, P.O. Box 500, Logan, Iowa 51546-0500.
Tel: 1-800-831-4190 • Fax: 1-800-543-2745
perfectionlearning.com
Paperback ISBN 0-7891-5880-9
Cover Craft® ISBN 0-7569-1105-2
1 2 3 4 5 6 PP 06 05 04 03 02

TABLE OF CONTENTS

Introduction 4

CHAPTER ONE
Record Breakers 6

CHAPTER TWO
Surprises! 20

CHAPTER THREE
Inspiring Athletes 31

CHAPTER FOUR
Olympic Trivia 49

Glossary 60

Index 63

Introduction

Every two years, athletes from all over the world gather for the Olympic Games. They take part in many different sports—from swimming to basketball, ice-skating to hockey.

Millions of people around the world watch the Games. They marvel at the incredible feats that the athletes perform.

The winners are given medals to honor their accomplishments. They win respect and praise for themselves, their teams, and their countries.

Every Olympics is special in its own way. Every time the Games are held, people see amazing athletic events. They come to know athletes whose stories inspire and delight. And sometimes spectators are treated to funny, unbelievable, and completely surprising moments.

This book takes a look at some of the Olympics' most interesting athletes. From record breakers to surprises, here are the moments that stand out in Olympic history.

CHAPTER ONE

Record Breakers

Setting and breaking records has always been part of Olympic history. Whenever the Games are held, new records are set in a variety of different events. From the hundreds of Olympic records, here are a few stories that are memorable.

The Man Who Could Fly

Track-and-field events have always been among the most popular and exciting competitions at the Olympics. Spectators enjoy watching men and women running fast, vaulting high, or jumping far. In track and field, records are often broken by tiny amounts. Just a fraction of an inch or a tenth of a second makes a difference. However, one track-and-field record wasn't just broken. It was smashed!

In 1968, the world's athletes gathered for the Summer Olympics in Mexico City,

The long jump track-and-field event

Mexico. As usual, the track-and-field events were very popular. Athletes from the United States did well in these events. But in the long jump, America's Bob Beamon almost didn't qualify.

During the long jump, an athlete runs down a track until he or she reaches a **foul line**. Then the athlete jumps forward as far as possible and lands in a sand pit. Officials measure the distance from the foul line to where the athlete landed. That determines how long the jump was. In 1968, the world record for the long jump was 27 feet 4 3/4 inches.

Beamon had trouble during the qualifying events for the long jump. During his first two attempts, he fouled because his toes were over the foul line when he started his jump. He had only one more chance.

Beamon's teammate, Ralph Boston, told him to start his jump several inches behind the line. Beamon was a strong jumper. Boston was sure Beamon would be able to qualify even if he started farther back.

Beamon took his teammate's advice. This time, he had no trouble qualifying for the finals.

Later that day, Beamon ran toward the long jump pit for the first round of the competition. He felt relaxed and confident. When he landed, he was almost at the end of the sand pit.

Beamon knew he had made a great jump. But he didn't know how good it was because everyone was talking about the distance in **meters**, not feet.

Beamon later recalled that he knew it was more than 27 feet 4 3/4 inches, which was the world record.

Then Ralph Boston told Beamon he thought the jump was over 29 feet.

Beamon replied in surprise, "What happened to 28 feet?"

A few minutes later, Beamon found out exactly how good his jump had been. He had jumped 29 feet 2 1/2 inches. This was almost 2 feet farther than the world record!

Bob Beamon receives his gold medal. Behind him are Ralph Boston and Klaus Beer.

Beamon was so excited, he began jumping up and down. Then he was overcome with emotion. He knelt down on the track and held his head in his hands.

No other competitor even came close to Beamon's incredible jump. Beamon won a gold medal for the long jump. He also set an Olympic record that still stands today.

The Perfect Gymnast

The 1976 Summer Games in Montreal, Canada, were filled with exciting events. But no competitor outshone a tiny teenager from Romania. Her name was Nadia Comaneci.

> **fun fact**
>
> In 1991, American Mike Powell beat Bob Beamon's long-jump record by more than 2 inches during a competition in Tokyo, Japan. Powell now holds the world record for the long jump. But Beamon's jump is still an Olympic record.

This gymnastics superstar performed routines that dazzled spectators and judges. She was so talented that she achieved the first perfect scores in the history of the Olympic Games. Not only was Comaneci perfect, she was perfect seven times!

Nadia Comaneci was born in Romania in 1961. When she was six years old, Romania's top gymnastic coach saw Comaneci playing on a school playground. He invited her to train with him.

Comaneci was a natural athlete. She took her sport very seriously. By the time she was 11 years old, she was the best gymnast in Romania.

In 1975, at the age of 14, Comaneci became the youngest person to win the European Championships. Her next challenge would be the Olympics.

On July 18, 1976, Comaneci marched into the **arena** in Montreal. She was only 4 feet 11 inches tall and weighed just 85 pounds. Her hair was tied back in pigtails held in place by red and white bows. She looked like a little girl, not a world-class athlete.

But when Comaneci stepped up to the uneven bars to do her **compulsory routine**, everyone realized that this was no child. Comaneci performed amazing tricks that no woman had ever done in competition. Her body flew through double twists, double backward somersaults, and other difficult moves. And she accomplished these moves with more style, strength, and confidence than any gymnast ever had.

When Comaneci finished her routine, the crowd burst into wild applause. Then they waited for the scores to be posted.

When the scoreboard finally flashed Comaneci's score, everyone was puzzled. The board read 1.0. One point was a ridiculously low score. It couldn't be right!

Then an announcer's voice came over the loudspeaker. He said that Nadia Comaneci had received a perfect score of 10.0.

That had never happened in the Olympics before. The scoreboard couldn't even show such a high number. That's why Comaneci's score had come up as 1.0.

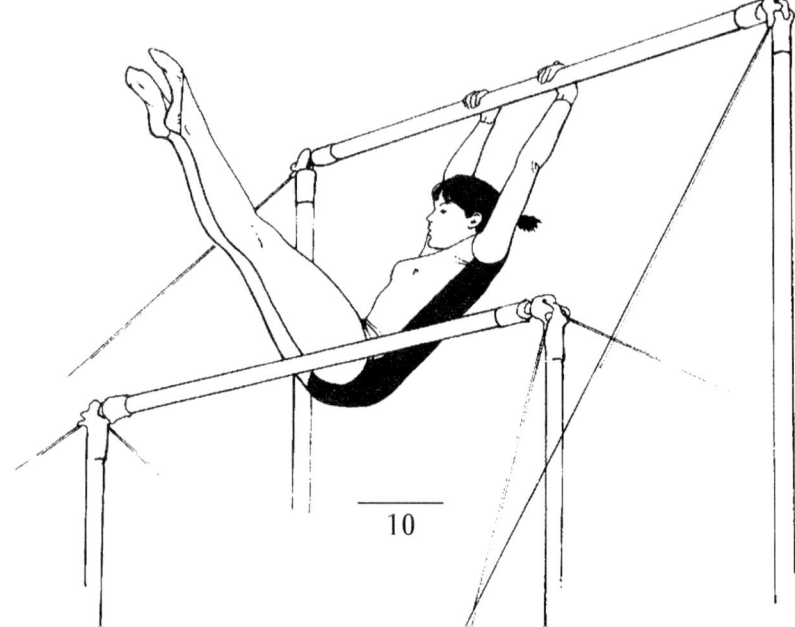

Comaneci didn't even look at the scoreboard. She had achieved perfect scores many times before in international competition. She knew her routine was perfect. She didn't even become excited. But everyone else in the arena was going wild.

The little gymnast from Romania went on to score three more perfect tens on the uneven bars. But she didn't stop there. The night after she scored her first perfect ten, Comaneci competed on the balance beam. During this event, gymnasts have 90 seconds to perform on a beam that is just 4 inches wide.

Comaneci's balance beam routine was just as amazing as her routine on the uneven bars. She confidently performed a handstand, several twirling dance steps, a back walkover, cartwheels, and splits. Then she jumped off the beam with a double twisting somersault.

Comaneci didn't make a single mistake. Once again, the scoreboard flashed a perfect score. Comaneci scored two more 10s on the beam later in the Olympics.

Comaneci ended up with seven perfect scores on the uneven bars and the balance beam during the 1976 Olympics. She achieved these scores in both team and **individual** events.

Comaneci also won three gold medals—for the balance beam, the uneven bars, and the best all-around gymnast. She won a bronze medal in the floor exercises and a silver medal as part of the Romanian team.

Comaneci's accomplishments didn't end at the 1976 Games. Her routines changed the face of gymnastics forever. Comaneci brought a new athleticism and style to the sport. She also inspired girls around the world to become gymnasts. Nadia Comaneci will always be remembered as the little girl who was perfect—seven times.

Swimming for Gold

The 1972 Summer Olympics in Munich, Germany, are usually remembered for a terrible tragedy. During the Games, **terrorists** took nine Israeli athletes **hostage**. Later, all the hostages, along with five terrorists and a German policeman, were killed in a gun battle.

Despite the tragedy of the 1972 Games, these Olympics also included amazing athletic events. One of the greatest accomplishments was achieved by U.S. swimmer Mark Spitz.

Mark Spitz's first swimming coach was his father. Arnold Spitz taught his son to swim when he was just a little boy growing up in California. Arnold Spitz was a demanding coach who was interested in just one thing. He told his son, "Swimming isn't everything; winning is."

Mark Spitz shared this attitude. As a result, most of his teammates thought he was **stuck-up** and **arrogant**. But they couldn't deny that Spitz was a terrific swimmer.

By the time he was in college, Spitz trained up to five hours a day. He had broken more than 35 records. Unlike many swimmers, Spitz learned different strokes instead of focusing on one style. He was also good at swimming both long and short distances.

Spitz's first Olympic experience was at the 1968 Games in Mexico City. The 18-year-old won two gold medals, plus one silver and one bronze. But Spitz was embarrassed. Before the Games, he had boasted that he would win six gold medals.

Spitz wanted things to be different at the 1972 Games. He entered four individual races—the 100-meter freestyle, the 200-meter freestyle, the 100-meter butterfly, and the 200-meter butterfly—and three team **relay** races.

This time, Spitz had nothing to be embarrassed about. Over eight days, he won a gold medal in every event he entered. He also set four world records. One German newspaper nicknamed Spitz "Mark the Shark."

But Mark Spitz almost didn't win all seven medals. He was so tired after the first five races that he asked his coach to take him out of the 100-meter freestyle.

Spitz thought that skipping one race would help him win the 4 x 100-meter medley relay later on. He also knew that his teammate, Jerry Heidenreich, had a good chance of beating him in the freestyle.

Spitz's coach told him that if he didn't swim the 100-meter race, everyone would say he didn't want to face Heidenreich. So Spitz swam the race. He beat Heidenreich to win his sixth gold medal. Then he won gold medal number seven in the 4 x 100-meter relay.

fun fact

Who held the world record for the 200-meter butterfly before Mark Spitz broke it at the Olympics? Mark Spitz! He had set the old record just a few weeks earlier at the Olympic trials.

Sadly, the terrorist attack on the Israeli athletes occurred just a few hours after Spitz won his seventh medal. Spitz was Jewish. He was afraid a terrorist might try to kill him too. Officials agreed. So Mark Spitz went home for his own safety.

Still, no one could take away his incredible accomplishment—seven gold medals in one Olympics. It is a record that still stands today.

A Perfect Pair

Ice dancing is one of the most dramatic sports at the Winter Games. This sport is like ballroom dancing on ice. Skaters dance to various types of music, such as the waltz or rock and roll. They are judged on their technical merit and their artistic impression. Strict rules prohibit spins, large jumps, or other athletic feats.

The dancers must skate together for most of their performance. This rule is important. Ice dancing is about two people dancing as one, not skaters performing spectacular moves. The most successful and dramatic pair of ice dancers in Olympic history is Jayne Torvill and Christopher Dean.

Ice dancing

Many competitive skaters begin lessons when they are very young. But Torvill and Dean were about ten years old when they started skating.

Both grew up in Nottingham, England. However, they did not meet until they were in their late teens. At that time, both Torvill and Dean were without partners. A coach suggested they work together. They did so well that a few months later, they came in second in their first competition.

Over the next few years, Torvill and Dean continued to win competitions. They spent hours training, despite the fact that both of them also had full-time jobs. Torvill worked as a secretary. Dean was studying to be a policeman.

Torvill and Dean went to the Olympics for the first time in 1980. That year, the Winter Games were held in Lake Placid, New York. The pair didn't win any medals. But they did place fifth in the competition.

The next Winter Olympics were held in 1984 in Sarajevo, Yugoslavia. By then, Torvill and Dean had won the European Championships three times and the World Championships four times. They had more perfect scores than any other pair in ice dancing history.

Torvill and Dean were the favorites to win the gold medal at the Olympics. And they did—in a way no other ice dancers had before.

During their compulsory routine, three of nine judges gave Torvill and Dean perfect scores of 6.0. Then they received four perfect scores during their short program.

On February 14, Torvill and Dean skated into the arena to perform their free dance. During this part of the competition, skaters are allowed to choose their own music. Torvill and Dean chose a classical piece, *Bolero*, by composer Maurice Ravel. *Bolero* is a romantic piece that starts simply and quietly, then builds to a dramatic ending.

The crowd could hardly believe their eyes as they watched Torvill and Dean skate. The pair skated together as if they were one being. Every move was perfect and beautiful. The routine cast a spell over everyone in the arena.

When the free dance ended, the fans leaped to their feet to applaud. Bouquets of flowers covered the ice. The spectators could not get enough of the skaters.

Finally, the scores were posted. Torvill and Dean received six 5.9s and three 6.0s for technical merit.

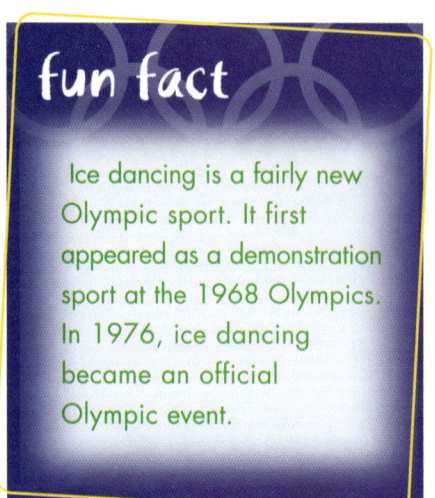

fun fact

Ice dancing is a fairly new Olympic sport. It first appeared as a demonstration sport at the 1968 Olympics. In 1976, ice dancing became an official Olympic event.

Even better, they received nine 6.0s for artistic impression. Torvill and Dean made Olympic history. And they set a new standard for all ice dancers to follow.

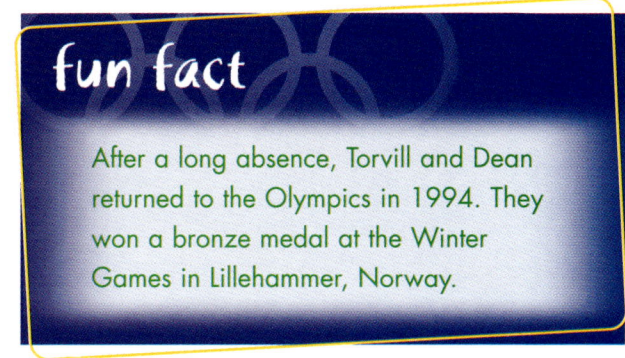

fun fact

After a long absence, Torvill and Dean returned to the Olympics in 1994. They won a bronze medal at the Winter Games in Lillehammer, Norway.

The World's Fastest Woman

Florence Griffith Joyner had an eye for style. Instead of wearing plain shorts and tank tops like other runners, Griffith Joyner wore colorful, one-legged bodysuits. She also had six-inch-long fingernails painted in a rainbow of colors.

But Griffith Joyner wasn't just stylish. She was an unbelievably fast runner who shattered Olympic records.

Florence Griffith was born in California in 1959. Her first Olympic appearance was at the 1984 Summer Olympics in Los Angeles. At those Games, she won a silver medal in the 200-meter dash. Her time of 22.04 seconds was only .01 second away from the Olympic record.

Griffith Joyner was determined to do even better at the 1988 Summer Games. These Games were held in Seoul, South Korea. Even though she was competing against many famous track stars, Griffith Joyner knew she could be the best runner there. Along with running, she did a lot of weight training to strengthen her leg muscles. Strong legs would allow her to burst out of the **starting blocks** at high speed.

In July 1988, Griffith Joyner had caused a sensation at the Olympic trials. These competitions determine which athletes will go on to the Olympic Games.

17

At the trials, Griffith Joyner had set a new world record. She had run the 100-meter dash in just 10.49 seconds. That was .27 seconds faster than the old record. Griffith Joyner had no trouble qualifying for the Olympics in the 100-meter and 200-meter dashes.

When the starting gun sounded for the 100-meter dash in Seoul, Griffith Joyner burst out of the blocks with explosive speed. She held the lead during the whole race and crossed the finish line 10.54 seconds later. Griffith Joyner had a huge smile on her face as she crossed the line. Her time set a new Olympic record.

The same thing happened in the 200-meter dash. Griffith Joyner's body was full of the sheer joy of running. She passed her competitors and took the lead. When she crossed the finish line 21.34 seconds later, she held the new world and Olympic records.

Griffith Joyner won two more medals at the 1988 Olympics. She helped her team win a gold medal in the 100-meter relay and a silver medal in the 400-meter relay.

Sadly, Griffith Joyner died in her sleep in 1998. She was only 38 years old. But Griffith Joyner will always be remembered as one of the most dramatic and fastest women in track-and-field history.

Florence Griffith Joyner

CHAPTER TWO

Surprises!

Many times, the winner of an Olympic event is easy to predict. Some athletes dominate a sport so much that it isn't a surprise when they win a gold medal. These athletes have already shown the world that they are the fastest, the strongest, or the best.

Sometimes, however, the results of Olympic competitions amaze everyone. It isn't only the famous athletes who stand on the podium wearing their medals. Throughout Olympic history, there have been several astonishing victories by athletes or teams who didn't seem to stand a chance. Here are three of the most surprising moments in Olympic history.

The Giant Killer

Spectators at the 2000 Summer Games in Sydney, Australia, had little doubt who would win the gold medal for Greco-Roman wrestling. Obviously, Alexander Karelin would be the champion. After all, the Russian wrestler already had three Olympic gold medals. He had not lost a match since 1987. And only one point had been scored against him during those 13 years. The Russian athlete was 6 feet 4 inches tall and weighed 286 pounds. He was a legend in the sport.

Karelin's opponent didn't seem to have much of a chance. He was Rulon Gardner, a 29-year-old man from the United States. Gardner was one of nine children. He grew up on a farm in Wyoming and spent his childhood milking cows and baling hay.

Gardner was so big that his classmates called him "Fatso" and "Blimp." But Gardner's size made him a powerful athlete. He was a star wrestler, football player, and shot-putter in high school. Then he was the U.S. national Greco-Roman heavyweight champion in 1995, 1997, and 2000.

Despite his strong record, Gardner didn't think he could beat Karelin at the 2000 Olympics. The two wrestlers had competed against each other before. In 1997, Karelin beat Gardner badly. Gardner later recalled that Karelin threw "me on my head three times."

On September 27, 2000, things would be different. Greco-Roman wrestling is a contest of **stamina** and skill. A wrestler uses his upper body to force his opponent to the mat. Wrestlers may lift their opponents and drop them to the mat. But they often spend most of the match pushing against each other or trying to stay on their feet.

When Karelin and Gardner faced each other in the ring, they pushed and grappled. Unlike their previous meeting, Karelin was unable to get Gardner in a position to throw him to the mat.

Instead, Gardner was able to tire his opponent by staying on his feet and keeping the pressure on. Finally, an **exhausted** Karelin let his hands slip apart. This move gave Gardner one point—and the gold medal. For the first time in 13 years, Karelin had lost a match.

Rulon Gardner (center) stands with his gold medal alongside silver medallist Alexander Karelin (right) of Russia and bronze medalist Dmitry Debelka of Belarus.

Gardner was so thrilled at winning that he turned a cartwheel. "Just think of the best dream you've ever had," he told an interviewer. "It's a hundred times better than that."

Gardner's upset became one of the most exciting and heartwarming stories of the 2000 Olympics. To honor his victory, the U.S. team gave Gardner the honor of carrying the U.S. flag during the closing ceremonies.

Gardner faced a new challenge in February 2002. He went out for a snowmobile ride and got lost. While trying to find his way home, Gardner fell in an icy river. He spent the night curled up in the snow, enduring temperatures that fell to 20° below zero. Gardner was rescued the next morning and flown to the hospital. His body temperature had dropped to 88°. Rescuers had to saw off his frozen boots. The young man's toes were frozen solid.

Gardner spent two weeks in the hospital. At first, doctors thought they would have to amputate his toes. However, although Gardner's toes were severely frostbitten, doctors were able to save all but one. Gardner faced months of physical therapy. And despite losing only one of his toes, he planned to keep wrestling and defend his title.

Miracle on Ice

In 1980, there was a lot of tension between the United States and the Soviet Union. Just a few months earlier, the Soviet army had invaded Afghanistan. This made the U.S. government so angry that it forced American athletes to **boycott** the 1980 Summer Games in Moscow, the capital of the Soviet Union.

But before the Summer Games were held, the 1980 Winter Olympics were scheduled for Lake Placid, New York. Athletes around the world gathered in the small town in February.

No one expected the United States to do very well at these Games. The Soviets, on the other hand, were expected to win a lot of medals. One medal they were sure to win was in hockey. In fact, the Soviets had won a gold medal in hockey at every Winter Olympics since 1964.

The American hockey team didn't have the talent or training that the Soviet team did. Soviet athletes were highly trained. Their living expenses were paid by the government. They were able to concentrate on their sport and nothing else. Soviet athletes also had the best coaches and training facilities.

Things didn't look good for the American team. It was made up of college and minor league players coached by Herb Brooks. He was the hockey coach at the University of Minnesota.

But Brooks was determined to turn his team into winners. His players weren't as talented or well-trained as the Soviets. Brooks knew the players would have to work twice as hard to make up for it.

Brooks trained his players hard. He made them skate up and down the ice to build their stamina and speed. He even had his players run laps. It was as if they were training for a track-and-field event instead of a hockey game.

Brooks had the team play games against college teams, foreign teams, and teams from the National Hockey League. The Americans won 42 out of 61 games. But they were also badly defeated by the Soviets 10–3. Would the same thing happen during the Olympics?

When the U.S. team arrived at Lake Placid, they were ranked number 7 out of the 12 Olympic teams. The teams were divided into two divisions.

The Americans' first game was against Sweden. Few people expected the Americans to win. Only a few thousand people turned out to see the game.

The U.S. team ended up coming from behind to tie the game. Even though they didn't win, the players were pleased that they had not given up even though they were losing.

Next the U.S. team faced Czechoslovakia. The Czechs took an early lead. The U.S. tied the game when Mike Eruzione scored a goal with 4 1/2 minutes left in the first period. Suddenly there was no stopping the Americans. They won the game 7 to 3. Instead of being **eliminated**, the Americans were tied with Sweden for first place in their division!

The U.S. team continued to surprise everyone. They won their next three games, beating Norway 5 to 1, Romania 7 to 2, and West Germany 4 to 2.

The Americans ended that first round with a record of 4–0–1. That was good enough to move on to the next round. The next two games would decide which team would go home with the gold medal.

America's first opponent in the next round was the dreaded Soviets. The two teams faced off against each other on February 22, 1980. More than 10,000 spectators watched. The Soviets had won all five games in their division. Everyone expected them to crush the American team.

Surprisingly, the U.S. hockey players weren't scared to face the mighty Soviet team. Instead, they were eager to take a shot at beating the Soviets. Coach Brooks encouraged this attitude by making jokes about the Soviet players. He didn't want his players to take their opponents too seriously.

The Americans fell behind early in the game 2 to 1. Then with just 1 second left in the first period, American Mark Johnson slipped a shot past the Soviet goalie. The score was tied.

During the second period, the Soviets made 12 shots, while the Americans only made two. Amazingly, goalie Jim Craig blocked all but one of the Soviets' shots. Still, the Soviets were leading, 3 to 2, when the teams came out for the third, and last, period.

The crowd in the Olympic Ice Center began to chant "U.S.A.! U.S.A.!" Then cheers filled the arena when Mark Johnson scored his second goal of the game to tie the score again.

Just over a minute later, the U.S. team's captain, Mike Eruzione, slammed the puck into the Soviet net from 30 feet away. The crowd—and the team—went wild. Eruzione was mobbed by his joyful teammates. The Americans were beating the "unbeatable" Soviets!

For the next ten minutes, the Soviets played sloppily. Craig had no trouble blocking their wild shots at the goal. As the last few seconds ticked away, the crowd began to cheer and wave American flags over their heads.

Finally, the buzzer sounded. The U.S. team had won! The American players crowded onto the ice. They hugged one another and threw their sticks into the air. The victory was so unexpected that the game came to be known as "the miracle on ice."

26

Two days after their stunning victory over the Soviet Union, the U.S. team took to the ice again. This time they faced a strong team from Finland. The winner of that game would go home with the gold medal.

Once again, the U.S. team did the impossible. They beat Finland 4 to 2. The U.S. hockey team had won the gold medal and shown the world that miracles really do happen.

At the 2002 Winter Games in Salt Lake City, Utah, members of the 1980 U.S. hockey team were given the honor of lighting the Olympic flame.

The American Olympic ice hockey team celebrates on the ice after defeating Finland.

The Runner Who Came Out of Nowhere

Few people had heard of Billy Mills before the 1964 Summer Games in Tokyo, Japan. But after those Olympics, the whole world was talking about this runner. He had come out of nowhere to win the 10,000-meter race.

William Mills was a Native American and a member of the Oglala Lakota Sioux tribe. He was born on the Pine Ridge Reservation in South Dakota in 1938. His mother died when he was seven. His father died a few years later.

Mills and his seven brothers and sisters were sent to a boarding school run by the U.S. government. Later, Mills attended the Haskell Indian School, a special high school for Native Americans. At Haskell, Mills joined several teams. One of those was the track team.

Mills discovered he was good at long-distance running. He won several state titles as a cross-country runner. His athletic ability led to a full **scholarship** at the University of Kansas.

Mills struggled with his schoolwork, but he kept on running track. He won several championships and tried out for the 1960 Olympics. He didn't make the team. Discouraged, Mills retired from running and joined the U.S. Marine Corps.

Mills tried to put running out of his mind, but he couldn't do it. He missed the track. His wife urged him to go back. So did his friends in the Marines.

Finally, Mills agreed. "I'd think to myself, you didn't retire, you quit," he explained. Soon after, he won a 10,000-meter race in Germany. Not long after that, Mills qualified for the U.S. Olympic Team.

When Mills entered the 10,000-meter race at the 1964 Summer Games in Tokyo, Japan, the odds against him were 1,000 to 1. Nobody expected him to even finish in the top ten. An Australian runner named Ron Clarke was the favorite.

On October 14, 1964, Mills, Clarke, and 36 other runners began the 10,000-meter race. The track was wet from a rainstorm earlier that morning.

As expected, Clarke stayed near the front of the pack for most of the race. But an American runner was keeping up with the leaders too. That American was Billy Mills.

The 10,000-meter race is 24 laps long. Each lap is almost 1/4 mile long.

After 16 laps, Clarke took the lead. Mills was right behind him. Sometimes Mills even managed to take the lead for a short time.

Mills stayed near the front of the pack until the 20th lap. Then the exhausted American began to fall back. By the 21st lap, Mills was 20 yards behind. Everyone believed he was finished.

Suddenly, something unexpected happened. Mills began to pick up speed. He drew closer and closer to Clarke and the other runners. As he ran, Mills' face twisted with pain from the tremendous effort.

At the beginning of the 24th and final lap, Clarke moved to his right to avoid another runner, Mohammed Gammoundi from Tunisia. Clarke bumped into Mills so hard that he knocked the American into another lane. As he paused to apologize, Gammoundi pushed his way between the other two runners. Gammoundi broke into the lead. Clarke sprinted after him. Mills followed.

It looked like Gammoundi would win the race. But Mills refused to give up. He sprinted desperately into the last 100 yards of the race. The crowd watch Gammoundi and Clarke. No one noticed Mills.

Suddenly, the American runner came out of nowhere. He passed Clarke with 30 yards to go. Ten yards later, he passed Gammoundi. Then Mills charged across the finish line. He had won the gold medal!

Mills also set an Olympic record by running the race in 28 minutes 24.4 seconds. That was more than 45 seconds faster than Mills had ever run the 10,000-meter race.

No one could believe that Mills had won. After he crossed the finish line, a puzzled Japanese official asked Mills, "Who are you?"

Later, Ron Clarke was asked if he had been worried about Mills before the race. The astonished Australian replied, "Worried about him? I never heard of him!"

Billy Mills entered the 10,000-meter race without any hope of winning. He finished as the only American to ever win the 10,000-meter race at the Olympics. Like many other Olympic athletes, he proved that the road to Olympic gold is full of surprises!

fun fact

The United States' first medal in the 10,000-meter race was also won by a Native American. In 1912, Hopi Indian Lewis Tewanima won a silver medal in the event.

CHAPTER THREE

Inspiring Athletes

Many people find winners inspiring. Stories of triumph are always exciting. But sometimes, athletes must overcome tremendous obstacles in order to achieve their dreams. Other athletes show us that winning is not as important as competing and doing your best. Here are a few athletes who showed the world the true meaning of success.

Running Against Racism

In 1936, the Summer Olympics were held in Berlin, the capital of Germany. Germany's ruler at that time was Adolf Hitler. Hitler and his Nazi Party believed that the white race was superior to all other races or **ethnic** groups. Hitler especially hated Jews and blacks. He called them inferior people.

Just three years later, Hitler would plunge Europe and most of the rest of the world into World War II. But in 1936, he wanted the Berlin Games to show everyone that white German athletes were better than all others.

There was just one problem with Hitler's plan. He hadn't counted on Jesse Owens. Owens was an African American track-and-field star on the U.S. team.

James Cleveland Owens was born on September 12, 1913, in Oakville, Alabama. His grandparents had been slaves. Owens was the 10th child of poor farmers. Later, the family moved to Cleveland, Ohio. Owens' father found work at a better-paying job in a steel mill there.

Owens always loved running. By the time he was in high school, he was a star on the track and basketball teams.

In 1933, Owens set several national high school records. He tied the high school world record for the 100-yard dash.

Owens continued his track-and-field success in college at Ohio State University. On May 25, 1935, Owens competed in a Big Ten college track meet. In just 45 minutes, Owens broke five world records and tied one more.

Newspapers called him "the world's fastest human." The next challenge for Owens was the 1936 Olympics.

In spite of the **racism** and hatred that Hitler and the Nazi Party felt toward nonwhite athletes, most of the German

Jesse Owens

people admired Owens. They cheered when he won the gold medal in the 100-meter dash. Hitler sat, angry and unsmiling, as he watched the African American steal the glory from his Nazi ideal.

Owens faced his greatest challenge during the broad jump competition a few days later. He was so aware of being a symbol for the black race that he tried too hard. He fouled the first two times he tried to qualify for the event. Then Owens received some help from an unlikely source—a German competitor named Luz Long.

Long had already qualified for the broad jump. He told Owens to draw a line a few inches behind the starting line and take off from there. That way, Owens would be sure not to foul. He would still jump far enough to qualify.

Owens knew that it took a lot of courage for Long to help an African American athlete—especially since Hitler was watching them from the stands. He thanked the German, did as he suggested, and had no trouble qualifying for the finals the next day.

Owens went on to win the broad jump and set an Olympic record of 26 feet 5 inches. Luz Long was the first person to congratulate Owens after his win.

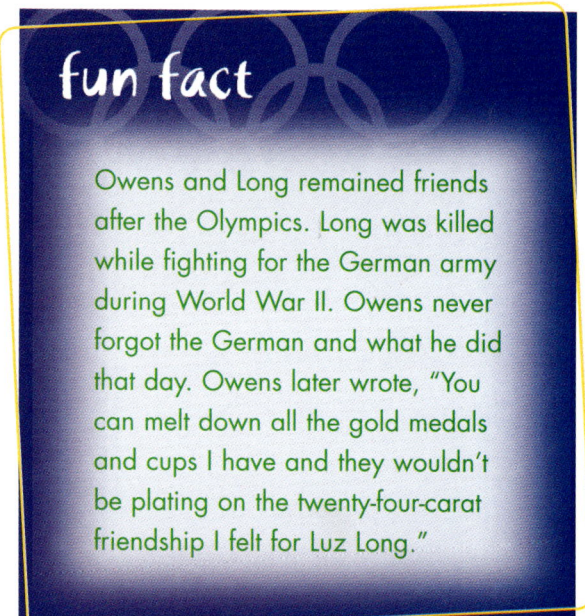

fun fact

Owens and Long remained friends after the Olympics. Long was killed while fighting for the German army during World War II. Owens never forgot the German and what he did that day. Owens later wrote, "You can melt down all the gold medals and cups I have and they wouldn't be plating on the twenty-four-carat friendship I felt for Luz Long."

Owens went on to win two more gold medals. One was in the 200-meter dash and the other in the 400-meter relay. He was the first athlete to win four gold medals at a single Olympics.

Owens returned home a great hero. However, he was unable to escape the racism and **segregation** in the United States.

> **fun fact**
>
> One of Owens' teammates at the Olympics was Mack Robinson. Robinson was the older brother of Jackie Robinson, who later became the first African American to play major-league baseball. Mack Robinson won a silver medal in the 200-meter dash—right behind Jesse Owens.

Because of his race, he had trouble making enough money to support himself and his family. At that time, job opportunities weren't offered to black athletes, no matter how much they had accomplished.

Just a few months after the Olympics ended, Owens began racing against horses. "It made me sick . . . [but] what was I supposed to do?" he said. "I had four gold medals, but you can't eat four gold medals."

Later when segregation ended and American society was more accepting of other races, Owens was able to make a good living as a public speaker and by making product **endorsements**.

Owens was awarded the Medal of Freedom by President Gerald Ford in 1976. In 1990, Owens was awarded the Congressional Medal of Honor by President George Bush. Even though

President George Bush

Owens died of lung cancer in 1980, he is still remembered as one of the most inspiring athletes at a very dark time in history.

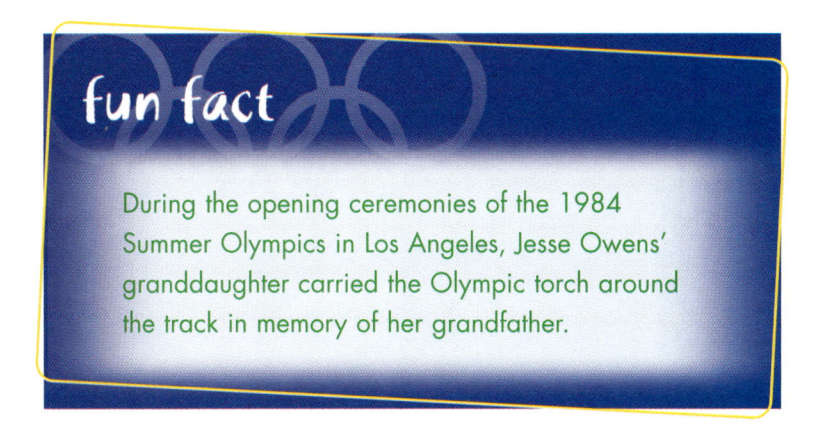

> **fun fact**
>
> During the opening ceremonies of the 1984 Summer Olympics in Los Angeles, Jesse Owens' granddaughter carried the Olympic torch around the track in memory of her grandfather.

The Symbol of a Nation

Australian track star Cathy Freeman was an unlikely person to become an Olympic hero. In fact, some people were surprised that she could even compete in the Games. These doubts were due to Freeman's ethnic background. She is an Aborigine. Aborigines are Australia's native people.

For centuries, Aborigines have been treated unfairly by the Australian government. They were forced to give up their land to European settlers.

Between 1910 and 1970, Aborigine children were taken away from their families and sent to European-style schools. These children later became known as "the stolen generation."

Aborigines began to win basic human rights in 1967. But even today, they are still a disadvantaged ethnic minority. Most Aborigines live in poverty. Their problems include unemployment, lack of health care, inadequate housing, poor schools, racial discrimination, and the loss of their native traditions.

Cathy Freeman was born in Mackay, Australia, in 1973. Her grandmother was a member of the stolen generation.

Like most Aborigine families, Freeman's family struggled to make a living and provide a good home for her. Despite the hardships, Freeman was an excellent athlete.

By the time she was 17 years old, she had become a champion **sprinter** and a member of Australia's national team. She was also named Young Australian of the Year.

Freeman wanted to use her fame to bring attention to the misfortunes of the Aborigines. She spoke out about racial injustice. She also visited schools and became a positive role model for children.

In 1994, Freeman won gold medals in the 200-meter and 400-meter races at the Commonwealth Games. The Commonwealth Games are open to athletes from Great Britain's former colonies.

Freeman wrapped the Australian and Aboriginal flags around herself during the celebrations. Some Australians criticized Freeman because they thought her actions were a political protest. But Freeman had only meant to show pride for her heritage. She realized that she was now a national symbol—for both Australia and the Aborigines.

Cathy Freeman

Freeman won a silver medal in the 400-meter race at the 1996 Summer Games in Atlanta. The next year, she became the first Aborigine to win an international track title when she took first place in the 400-meter race at the IAAF World Championships in Athens, Greece.

In 2000, Sydney, Australia, hosted the Summer Games. As at every Olympics, the host nation had to choose someone to light the Olympic flame. On September 15, 2000, millions of people around the world watched Freeman light the Olympic flame at the opening ceremonies. It was a tremendous honor.

Ten days later, Freeman represented her country again. This time she was on the field. Freeman competed in the 400-meter race. And she won the gold medal!

Freeman fell to the track in relief after she crossed the finish line. She later said the pressure of the moment was overwhelming.

Freeman had not only won the race for herself. She had also represented Australia and her Aboriginal people. Later, she proudly told reporters, "My accomplishments at the Olympics have helped to bring the **indigenous** community and the white community in my country together."

Running Blind

Imagine running a race even though you can barely see what's in front of you. Then imagine winning races and competing at the Olympics! That's exactly the story of U.S. middle-distance runner Marla Runyan.

Marla Runyan was born in 1969 in Camarillo, California. She was an active, athletic child. But when she was nine years old, she began to have trouble seeing. Everything in the middle of her vision was a dark blur. Runyan had a **degenerative** disease that was destroying her eyes' **retinas**. Soon she was legally blind.

Although Runyan can't see what's in front of her, she still has peripheral vision. That means she can see things to the side. This ability helped her continue running in several different track-and-field events.

Marla Runyan

    Runyan has said that what's in front of her disappears into a hole. But she can still see the track under her feet. She also figures out which runners are the ones to beat, then memorizes their uniform colors and hairstyles so she can see where they are on the track. And Runyan's coach thinks that not being able to see well helps her focus on the race without becoming distracted.

    In 1992 and 1996, Runyan won five gold medals in the **Paralympic** Games for disabled athletes. But she wanted to compete with nondisabled athletes as well.

    Runyan qualified for the Olympic trials in the **heptathlon**. Although she didn't make the team, she did set a U.S. record in the 800-meter race, the final event of the heptathlon.

In 1999, Runyan won the 1,500-meter race at the Pan Am Games. That year, she was also ranked number two out of all U.S. runners in the 1,500-meter race.

Then in 2000, she achieved her greatest dream. Runyan competed as part of the U.S. Olympic team at the Summer Games in Sydney. She knew it was unlikely that she would win the 1,500-meter race, but she still ran her best.

Marla Runyan didn't win the 1,500-meter race. She came in eighth place. However, this was a great accomplishment. Runyan and other Americans were proud of her achievements. "I guess I'm demonstrating the possibilities that the sighted never imagined were possible," she said to an interviewer after the race.

A Dream Come True

When Wilma Rudolph was growing up in Tennessee, no one ever would have expected her to be an Olympic champion. The little girl had always been sickly. She could barely walk. Yet when she was 20, this unlikely athlete not only competed in the Olympics, she won three gold medals!

Wilma Rudolph weighed only 4 1/2 pounds when she was born in Clarksville, Tennessee, in 1940. She was two months **premature**. She was the 20th of 22 children. Rudolph's family was so poor, the children had to wear clothes made out of old flour sacks.

Life continued to be hard for Rudolph and her family. Rudolph was so weak that she later wrote she was "the sickest child in Clarksville."

When she was four years old, Rudolph almost died from pneumonia and scarlet fever. Then she became ill with polio. This disease often leaves victims unable to walk or move. Polio paralyzed Rudolph's left leg. Doctors said she would never walk again.

To help Rudolph recover, she and her mother took the bus 50 miles to Nashville, Tennessee, twice a week. In a hospital for African Americans, Rudolph received **massages** and did exercises to strengthen her leg. She also had to wear a brace with a special shoe.

At first, Rudolph felt sorry for herself. Then she got angry. She decided that she didn't want to be paralyzed for the rest of her life. She worked as hard as she could to recover.

Finally when she was 11 years old, Rudolph was able to walk without wearing her leg brace. One of the proudest days of her life was when her mother packed up the brace and mailed it back to the Nashville hospital.

Rudolph was so excited to be walking again that she started running. Her parents encouraged her to be athletic so she could strengthen her body and overcome her physical problems.

Rudolph joined the basketball and track teams in high school. She soon got the nickname "Skeeter," because her coach said she buzzed around like a mosquito.

By 1956, when she was 16, Rudolph ran fast enough to qualify for the Summer Olympics in Melbourne, Australia. At those Games, she won a bronze medal as part of the U.S. 4 x 100-meter relay team.

But Rudolph's greatest moment came four years later at the 1960 Summer Games in Rome, Italy. Even though she sprained her ankle just one day before the race, she won the 100-meter race in 11 seconds. She then went on to win the 200-meter race in 24 seconds. She also helped the U.S. team win a gold medal in the 4 x 100-meter relay.

Reporters called her "the fastest woman in the world." Rudolph had come a long way from the sickly child who could barely walk!

After the Olympics, Rudolph worked as a teacher and a coach. She also ran a community center and started a foundation to provide books to poor children.

Rudolph died in 1994 of a brain tumor. But her determination and courage continue to inspire athletes around the world.

> **fun fact**
>
> When Rudolph returned home to Clarksville, the mayor wanted to give her a victory parade. In those days, Clarksville, like other Southern towns, was segregated. Rudolph refused to take part in the parade unless both blacks and whites could attend. The mayor agreed. Rudolph's victory parade and **banquet** were the first nonsegregated events in Clarksville's history.

The Pressure of the Past

Dan Jansen was one of the favorites to win the 500-meter speed skating race at the 1988 Winter Olympics in Calgary, Canada. But that morning, Jansen had received terrible news. His big sister, Jane, had died of leukemia.

Jansen thought he could put Jane's death out of his mind during the race. Athletes are trained to focus on their performance and nothing else. But Jansen could not concentrate on the race. He skated slowly. Then he fell. Jansen had lost his chance to win a medal.

Four days later, Jansen competed in the 1,000-meter race. This time, he got off to a good start. But as he passed the 800-meter mark, he fell. Once again, he lost the race.

People all over the world **sympathized** with Jansen. After the Olympics, Jansen received more than 7,000 letters from people who had been touched by his story. Most of the letters encouraged him to try again.

In 1992, Jansen tried to reach his Olympic dreams again at the Winter Games in Albertville, France. Once again, he was favored to win the 500-meter race. Surely, this time, Jansen would succeed!

But once again, Jansen fell short of his goal. The ice on the track was soft and bumpy. Jansen completed the race without falling, but he finished fourth.

Jansen did even worse in the 1,000-meter race. His loss in the 500-meter race upset him so much, he thought there was no way he could win the 1,000-meter race either. Jansen later admitted that he was not mentally or physically prepared to win. Instead, he finished in 26th place.

Because of a change in the Olympic schedule, the next Winter Olympics were held just two years later in Lillehammer, Norway. Jansen knew this would be his last Olympics—and his last chance at a medal.

This time, Jansen felt more **motivated** than ever to succeed. By the time he arrived at Lillehammer, he was considered the best 500-meter and 1,000-meter skater in the world. But once again, it seemed that Jansen would be remembered as the man who could not win an Olympic medal.

The 500-meter race was held on February 14, 1994. That was exactly six years after Jansen's sister had died and he had fallen in the 500-meter race in Calgary.

Jansen got a good start in the 500-meter race. But as he skated, Jansen could feel that his skates were not gripping the ice. Still, he skated as hard and as fast as he could.

Suddenly, the unthinkable happened. As Jansen approached the last turn, his left skate slipped. His hand touched the ice.

Dan Jansen holds daughter Jane after receiving the gold medal for speed skating.

Although he didn't fall, the accident caused Jansen to lose precious time. He finished the race in eighth place.

Once again, people all over the world felt sorry for Jansen. The skater also felt terrible. His confidence was gone. He felt he didn't have a chance in the 1,000-meter race four days later. But he decided to compete anyway.

Jansen tried to put the 500-meter race out of his mind. His only focus was the 1,000-meter race.

When the starting gun went off on February 18, Jansen took off. He settled into a good rhythm and skated with smooth, powerful strokes.

Suddenly, on the second-to-last turn, Jansen slipped. His left hand reached for the ice. The crowd gasped. Was Jansen going to fall again? Would his last chance at a medal end in disaster, as it had so many times before?

But Jansen stayed calm. He recovered his balance and kept skating. The crowd roared as he exploded across the finish line. Jansen's time was 1 minute 12.43 seconds. It was Jansen's best time ever in the 1,000-meters. It was also a world record! Best of all, it gave Jansen the Olympic gold medal.

Jansen later wrote that he never knew how good winning would feel. Even more importantly, he had shown the world that if a person never gives up, he or she always has a chance to succeed.

Performing While Injured

Gymnasts often compete when they are injured. In 1972, Japanese gymnast Shun Fujimoto broke his leg during his floor exercise routine. He did not tell his teammates or coach about the injury so he could keep competing.

Fujimoto scored a 9.5 on the pommel horse and a 9.7 on the rings after his leg injury. When he dismounted from the rings, Fujimoto had to land on both feet. He did—but **dislocated** his knee.

Fujimoto burst into tears from the pain and finally admitted his injury. He could no longer compete. But his points helped the Japanese team win a gold medal. The team dedicated their victory to Fujimoto.

Kerri Strug was another gymnast who refused to let her team down when she was injured. She competed in the 1996 Summer Olympics in Atlanta. Strug, her teammates, and Coach Bela Karolyi were determined to bring home a gold medal for the United States. But they knew it would be hard to defeat the powerful Russian team.

After the first night of competition, the U.S. trailed the first-place Russians by .127 of a point. The scores remained close during the second night of competition.

The vault was the last event for the United States. The team that won this event would win the gold medal. Each gymnast was allowed two vaults. But only the higher score counted.

Strug was the last member of the U.S. team to vault. She ran toward the horse and performed a difficult vault with a twist. But when she landed, Strug heard her left ankle pop. Pain shot up her leg.

Strug's ankle hurt so much, she wasn't sure she could perform her second vault. In the past, she might have let the injury knock her out of the competition. But she couldn't let her team down. So Strug limped to the end of the runway. Then she forgot about the pain and performed her second vault.

This time, when Strug landed, she heard her ankle snap. She balanced on her good leg for a moment. Then she fell to her knees in pain.

As her trainers helped Strug off the floor, her score appeared on the scoreboard. It was a 9.712. The U.S. team had won the gold medal!

Kerri Strug on her knees in pain after her landing

Strug had torn two **ligaments** in her ankle. The photo of her coach carrying her to the podium to accept her gold medal with the rest of her teammates became one of the most popular images from the Atlanta Olympics.

Spectators at the 1968 Summer Games in Mexico City saw another display of courage and determination. That year, the **marathon** was won by Mamo Wolde of Ethiopia. But the high point of the race came more than an hour later. That's when the last runner, John Stephen Akhwari of Tanzania entered the **stadium**. Akhwari could barely walk. His right leg was bloody and bandaged.

As he made his painful way around the track, the crowd began to clap. When Akhwari finally crossed the finish line, the crowd cheered as loudly as they had for the winner. Later, Akhwari seemed surprised at all the fuss. He told reporters, "I don't think you understand. My country did not send me to Mexico City to start the race. They sent me to finish the race."

Overcoming the Odds

Elizabeth Robinson was another athlete who overcame incredible odds to win a gold medal. Robinson was only 16 years old when she took part in the 1928 Olympics in Amsterdam. Although she had competed in her first track meet just four months before the Olympics, the teenager not only won a gold medal in the 100-meter sprint, she also set a world record.

In 1931, Robinson was in a terrible plane crash. She was so badly injured that rescuers thought she was dead. Robinson was in a coma for two months because of serious head injuries. Her leg was so badly injured that no one expected her to walk again. But Robinson surprised everybody. She competed in the 1936 Olympics in Berlin and won the gold medal as a member of the 4 x 100-meter relay team!

CHAPTER FOUR

Olympic Trivia

The Olympics have had a large number of surprises, odd events, and little-known facts. Here are some interesting stories and trivia from the Olympic Games.

Superlatives

- Edward Eagan from the United States is the only person to win gold medals at both the Summer and Winter Games. In 1920, Eagan won a gold medal for light-heavyweight boxing at the Summer Games in Antwerp, Belgium. Then he was part of the four-man bobsled team that won gold at the 1932 Winter Games in Lake Placid, New York.

- Christa Rothenburger-Luding of East Germany is the only athlete who won medals at the Summer and Winter Games in the same year. She won a gold and a silver medal for speed skating at the 1988 Winter Games in Calgary, Canada. Then she won a silver medal in the women's sprint cycling event at the Summer Olympics in Seoul, South Korea.

- The youngest person to win an Olympic gold medal was an unnamed French boy who was part of the Dutch rowing team at the 1900 Games in Paris, France. The boy was between seven and ten years old.

The youngest gold medalist who is known by name was Kim Yoon-mi, a 13-year-old from South Korea. She won the women's short-track speed skating relay event at the 1994 Winter Games in Lillehammer, Norway.

- The oldest person to win an Olympic gold medal was Oscar Swahn of Sweden. He was 64 years old when he won his medal at the 1912 Games in Stockholm, Sweden. Swahn's team took part in an unusual event called the running deer shooting single-shot. This event is no longer held!

fun fact

Oscar Swahn also holds the record for the oldest Olympic competitor. He competed in the 1920 Games when he was 72 years old.

- American Mark Spitz won seven gold medals for swimming at the 1972 Summer Games in Munich, Germany. This was the most gold medals won by one person at a single Olympics. Spitz won his medals for three individual events and four team events.

- U.S. speed skater Eric Heiden won the most individual gold medals—five—at the 1980 Winter Games in Lake Placid, New York.

- U.S. athlete Ray Ewry won the most gold medals in history. He won ten medals for track-and-field events at the Summer Games in 1900, 1904, and 1908.

- The most medals won by a single person is 18. Russian gymnast Larissa Latynina won 9 gold, 5 silver, and 4 bronze medals at the Summer Olympics in 1956, 1960, and 1964.

- Hubert Raudaschl of Austria competed in a record nine Summer Olympics in 1964, 1968, 1972, 1976, 1980, 1984, 1988, 1992, and 1996. He was a member of the yachting team.

Olympians Big and Small

- The smallest Olympic athlete was figure skater Sonja Henie of Norway. Eleven-year-old Henie was only 4 feet 3 inches tall and weighed 60 pounds when she competed at the 1924 Winter Games in Chamonix, France. She won gold medals at the 1928, 1932, and 1936 Games. Henie later became a popular movie star.
- The tallest Olympian was a Russian basketball player named Yanis Kruminsch. He was 7 feet 3 inches tall when he played at the 1960 Summer Games in Rome, Italy.
- The heaviest Olympic athlete was Chris Taylor, a weightlifter from the United States. At the 1972 Summer Games in Munich, Germany, Taylor weighed between 401 and 419 pounds and won a bronze medal in his event.

Royal Athletes

Even royalty can be part of the Olympics.
- Crown Prince Olav of Norway won a gold medal at the 1928 Olympics. He was a member of Norway's yachting team. Twenty-nine years later, the prince became king of Norway.
- In 1960, Crown Prince Constantin of Greece won a gold medal as a member of the sailing team. He later became king of Greece.
- Princess Anne of Great Britain took part in an **equestrian** event at the 1976 Summer Games in Montreal, Canada. She is the daughter of Queen Elizabeth II of England.

- Prince Albert of Monaco was a member of that country's 4-man bobsled team at five Winter Olympics in 1988, 1992, 1996, 1998, and 2002.

Prince Albert of Monaco carries the Olympic Flame during the 2002 Winter Olympic Torch Relay.

Equality on the Field

Equestrian and shooting events are the only two sports in the Olympics where men and women compete against each other.

Wacky Olympic Sports

The sports watched in today's Olympic Games aren't the only events that are part of Olympic history. The first few modern Games had some events that seem downright silly today. These are some of the more unusual Olympic events of the past.

- At the 1900 Olympic Games in Paris, France, athletes competed in a 200-meter obstacle course. Competitors dove into the polluted Seine River, climbed over a pole, rushed over a row of boats, and swam under another row of boats.
- The 1900 Games in Paris featured live pigeon shooting.
- The 1904 Olympic Games in St. Louis, Missouri, featured "the plunge for distance." During this event, competitors dove into a pool and glided underwater as far as they could before they had to come up for air.
- The 1906 interim Olympic games included a dueling pistols contest. Competitors shot at mannequins dressed in long coats. Each mannequin had a bull's-eye painted on its throat.

- The 1906 Games also featured an event called the stone throw. The winner was the competitor who could throw a 14-pound rock the farthest.
- The cross-country race at the 1924 Summer Games in Paris was such a disaster that the event was never held again. One-third of the 38 runners collapsed in the 110° heat. Several had to be rushed to the hospital. Other runners got lost on the wooded course and had to be rescued by the Red Cross.
- Tug-of-war was an Olympic event until 1920.

fun fact

In 1908, teams of British policemen came in first, second, and third in the tug-of-war competition.

Polo

- Gymnastic events used to include rope climbing and club swinging.
- Croquet, golf, lacrosse, polo, rugby, and motorboating have all been Olympic sports.

How Does a Sport Become Part of the Olympics?

It takes many years for a sport to join the Olympic family. To qualify, a men's sport must be played in at least 75 countries on 4 continents. For women, a sport must be played in at least 40 countries on 3 continents.

Once a sport is accepted, it appears as a demonstration sport. Athletes compete in the sport, but they aren't awarded any medals. A sport may make several appearances as a demonstration sport before it finally becomes a regular Olympic event.

fun fact

Several new sports have been added to the Olympics over the past few years. Trampolining and the triathlon are two. These events appeared as official sports for the first time at the 2000 Summer Games in Sydney, Australia.

The 2002 Winter Games in Salt Lake City, Utah, featured one new sport—women's bobsledding—and the return of the skeleton, a downhill sledding event, which had last been in the Olympics in 1948.

Becoming an Olympic Athlete

How does a person become an Olympic athlete? Most sports include qualifying events, or trials. At the trials, the top athletes win the chance to represent their country at the Olympics.

Some athletes are chosen through a ranking system. For example, the U.S. ski team is made up of members of the U.S. Ski and Snowboard Association (USSA).

USSA members can compete in more than 3,000 events in the U.S. each year. Competitors are ranked according to how well they do. The top finishers are invited to join the U.S. team at the next Winter Games.

The Pan Am Games are an international event that determines which teams go to the Olympics in some sports. During the 1999 Pan Am Games, for example, the top two baseball teams, U.S.A. and Cuba, qualified for the 2000 Olympics in Sydney. The winner of the field hockey championships also won the right to go to Sydney. Some individual sports, such as water polo, triathlon, and rhythmic gymnastics, send the top Pan Am finishers to the Olympics.

An Unusual Olympic Record

John Lucas has run at every Olympic Games since 1952, except the boycotted 1980 Games in Moscow, Soviet Union. But this runner, who was 74 years old when he appeared at the 2000 Summer Games in Sydney, Australia, isn't part of any official event. Instead, he arrives a day or two before the Games begin. Then he slips into the stadium and runs his own 10,000-meter race. His time in 2000 was 61 minutes. That was 34 minutes longer than the gold-medal winner's time.

Tarzan at the Olympics?

Many athletes have appeared in movies or on television shows after they won Olympic glory. The most successful athlete-turned-actor was Johnny Weissmuller.

Weissmuller won three gold medals in swimming at the 1924 Summer Games in Paris, France. In 1928, he won two more gold medals at the Amsterdam Summer Olympics.

During his swimming career, Weissmuller set 28 world records. Afterward, Weissmuller starred as Tarzan in 12 popular movies. Olympic medalists Buster Crabbe, Glenn Morris, and Herman Brix also played Tarzan in the movies. Crabbe won gold in the 400-freestyle in 1932. Brix won a silver medal in the shot put in 1928. Morris won gold in the decathlon in 1936.

Small Country, Big Honors

At the Summer Olympics in 1976, Hasely Crawford of the tiny country of Trinidad and Tobago surprised everyone when he won a gold medal in the men's 100-meter race. Crawford became a huge hero and received many honors when he returned home. Trinidad and Tobago issued a stamp in his honor. A plane was named after him, and many songs were written about his victory.

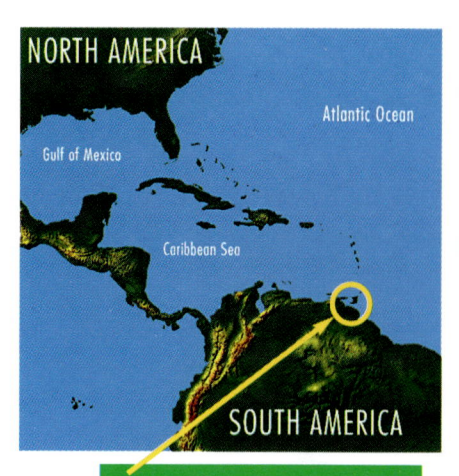

Trinidad and Tobago

Family Affairs

Some Olympic medals are a family affair. Between 1908 and 1924, Sweden's Oscar Swahn and his son Alfred won six gold, four silver, and five bronze medals in **sharpshooting**.

In 1968 and 1976, Australian Bill Roycroft and his son Wayne won bronze medals as part of the three-day equestrian team event.

Perhaps the most remarkable Olympic family is the Sheas. In 1932, Jack Shea won 2 gold medals in speed skating at the Lake Placid Games. His son, Jimmy Shea, competed in three events with the U.S. ski team at the 1964 Games.

fun fact

There have been several brothers or sisters who have competed in the Olympics. A few of these family competitors are Phil and Steve Mahre (skiing), Leon and Michael Spinks (boxing), and Venus and Serena Williams (tennis).

Then in 2002, Jack Shea's grandson, Jim, won a gold medal in the skeleton at the Salt Lake City Games. The Sheas are the only three-generation Olympic family. Sadly, Jack Shea was killed in a car accident just before the 2002 Games, so he was unable to see his grandson make Olympic history.

> **fun fact**
>
> Spectators at the 1980 Summer Games must have thought they were seeing double! Twin brothers Bernd and Jorg Landvoigt of East Germany won the gold medal in a rowing race called the pair-oared shell. The silver medal was won by a set of twins, Yuri and Nikolai Pimenov, from the Soviet Union.

Glossary

arena area surrounded by seating for spectators, where sports events or shows take place

arrogant feeling or displaying self-importance

banquet elaborate formal meal attended by many guests. It is often held in honor of a particular person or occasion.

boycott to refuse to take part in an event in order to protest a group or action

compulsory routine in gymnastics and skating, a series of moves that every competitor has to complete

degenerative relating to a disease that causes a steady decline in health

dislocate to move or force a bone out of the joint in which it fits

eliminate to defeat and put a player or team out of a competition

endorsement act of publicly supporting the use of a product

equestrian relating to horseback riding

ethnic relating to large groups of people classed according to common racial, national, tribal, religious, or cultural origins

exhausted extremely tired

foul line boundary line beyond which a player is not permitted to step

heptathlon athletic contest, often for women, in which each contestant must compete in seven track-and-field events

hostage person taken by force to secure the taker's demands

indigenous having originated in a particular region or environment

individual intended for one person

ligament sheet or band of tough tissue that connects bones or cartilage at a joint

marathon long-distance race of 26 miles and 385 yards

massage treatment that involves rubbing or kneading the muscles

meter basic unit of length that equals about 39.37 inches

motivated having enough interest or incentive to do something

Paralympic Games Olympics for disabled athletes, held immediately after the Olympics at the same site

premature relating to being born before expected development is completed

racism belief that one race of people is better than all other races

relay race in which members of a team take turns competing until the race is completed

retina light-sensitive membrane in the back of the eye containing rods and cones that receive an image from the lens and send it to the brain through the optic nerve

scholarship award that pays for higher education

segregate to separate by class, race, religion, or sex

sharpshooting act of using firearms to accurately hit a target

sprint to run a short distance at a high speed

stadium place where people watch sports or other activities. It is usually a large enclosed flat area surrounded by tiers of seats for spectators

stamina enduring physical or mental energy and strength that allows somebody to do something for a long time

starting blocks pair of objects used by runners to brace their feet against at the start of a sprint race

stuck-up snobbish

sympathize to share the feelings of somebody else or show pity or compassion for another

terrorist person who uses violence or the threat of violence to intimidate, often for political purposes

Index

Akhwari, John Stephen, 47–48
Beamon, Bob, 7–9
Boston, Ralph, 7, 8
Brix, Herman, 57
Brooks, Herb, 24, 25
Clarke, Ron, 29–30
Comaneci, Nadia, 9–11
Crabbe, Buster, 57
Craig, Jim, 26
Crawford, Hasely, 58
Dean, Christopher, 15–17
Eagan, Edward, 49
Eruzione, Mike, 25, 26
Ewry, Ray, 50
Freeman, Cathy, 35–38
Fujimoto, Shun, 45–46
Gammoundi, Mohammed, 29–30
Gardner, Rulon, 21–23
Griffith Joyner, Florence, 17–19
Heiden, Eric, 50
Heidenreich, Jerry, 14
Henie, Sonja, 51
Hitler, Adolf, 31, 32, 33
Jansen, Dan, 42–45
Johnson, Mark, 26

Karelin, Alexander, 20–21, 23
Kruminsch, Yanis, 51
Landvoigt, Bernd, 59
Landvoigt, Jorg, 59
Latynina, Larissa, 50
Long, Luz, 33
Lucas, John, 56
Mahre, Phil, 58
Mahre, Steve, 58
Mills, Billy, 28–30
Morris, Glenn, 57
Owens, Jesse, 31–35
Pimenov, Nikolai, 59
Pimenov, Yuri, 59
Powell, Mike, 9
Raudaschl, Hubert, 51
Robinson, Elizabeth, 48
Robinson, Mack, 34
Rothenburger-Luding, Christa, 49
royalty
    Crown Prince Constantin, 51
    Crown Prince Olav, 51
    Prince Albert, 52
    Princess Anne, 51
Roycroft, Bill, 58

Roycroft, Wayne, 58
Rudolph, Wilma, 40–42
Runyan, Marla, 38–40
Shea, Jack, 58–59
Shea, Jim, 59
Shea, Jimmy, 58
Spinks, Leon, 58
Spinks, Michael, 58
Spitz, Mark, 13–14, 50
Strug, Kerri, 46–47
Swahn, Alfred, 58
Swahn, Oscar, 50, 58

Taylor, Chris, 51
Tewanima, Lewis, 30
Torvill, Jayne, 15–17
United States Olympic hockey
    team, 24–27
Weissmuller, Johnny, 57
Williams, Serena, 58
Williams, Venus, 58
Wolde, Mamo, 47
Yoon-mi, Kim, 50

Library
Renfroe Middle School
220 W. College Ave.
Decatur, GA 30030